This edition published in 2018 by Arcturus Publishing Limited
26/27 Bickels Yard, 151–153 Bermondsey Street,
London SE1 3HA, UK

Copyright © Arcturus Holdings Limited

All rights reserved. No part of this publication may be reproduced, stored in a retrieval system, or transmitted, in any form or by any means, electronic, mechanical, photocopying, recording, or otherwise, without prior written permission in accordance with the provisions of the Copyright Act 1956 (as amended). Any person or persons who do any unauthorized act in relation to this publication may be liable to criminal prosecution and civil claims for damages.

Illustrated by Jean Claude
Written by Paul Virr
Edited by Anne Peebles and Donna Gregory
Designed by Square and Circus

ISBN: 978-1-78828-672-5
CH006242NT
Supplier 29 Date 0918 Print run 6976

Printed in China

DRAW WITH CRAYONS!

This book shows you how to make fun pictures with wax crayons. Below are the different ways they are used in this book. Come back to this page if you need to check how to do something.

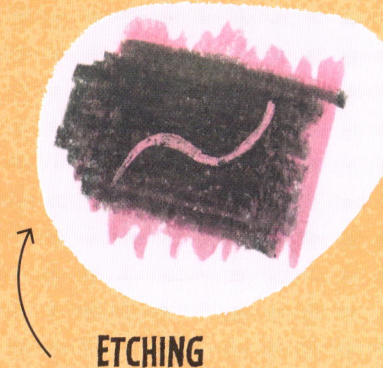

ETCHING
Make a layer of one crayon, and cover it with a thick black layer. Use a safe, pointed tip (like a pencil) to scratch lines on top to reveal what's underneath.

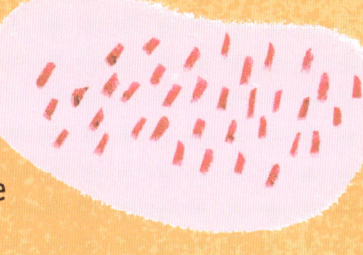

STIPPLING
Use the top edge of the crayon to make dots.

SHADING
Shade from dark to light by pressing firmly, then gently.

TEXTURE RUBBING
Lay a textured surface under your paper and rub with a crayon. See what great effects you can get—try using clothes, bark, carpets, walls, or leaves. Just be careful to keep the crayon on the paper!

CIRCLES
Twirl the flat end of the crayon for circular shapes.

DOUBLING UP
See what happens when you hold two crayons together.

Turn the page to begin!

Rainy Day Fun

Make short strokes for raindrops with the crayon point. Then add more with another crayon... and another. Now you have a lovely shower!

Quick, put up your umbrella! Make a pink outline in a half-circle, divide it in sections, and fill it in. Add a handle and you'll be quite dry!

Make it rain even more so that the children can splash about. Add umbrellas for everyone too!

Fun Fireworks

Make sparkly fireworks explode by etching (see p.3). Merge several different shades together, then go over them with black. Scratch out spiral, star, and swirly shapes.

Fill the sky with fantastic fireworks.

Chilly Snowman

Begin with a simple oval. Lay the picture over a textured surface, then fill in the white with the side of the crayon. Add details with the crayon tips.

Super Skaters

Make loops, zigzags, and wavy lines, first with one crayon, then two to match the skaters' two feet.

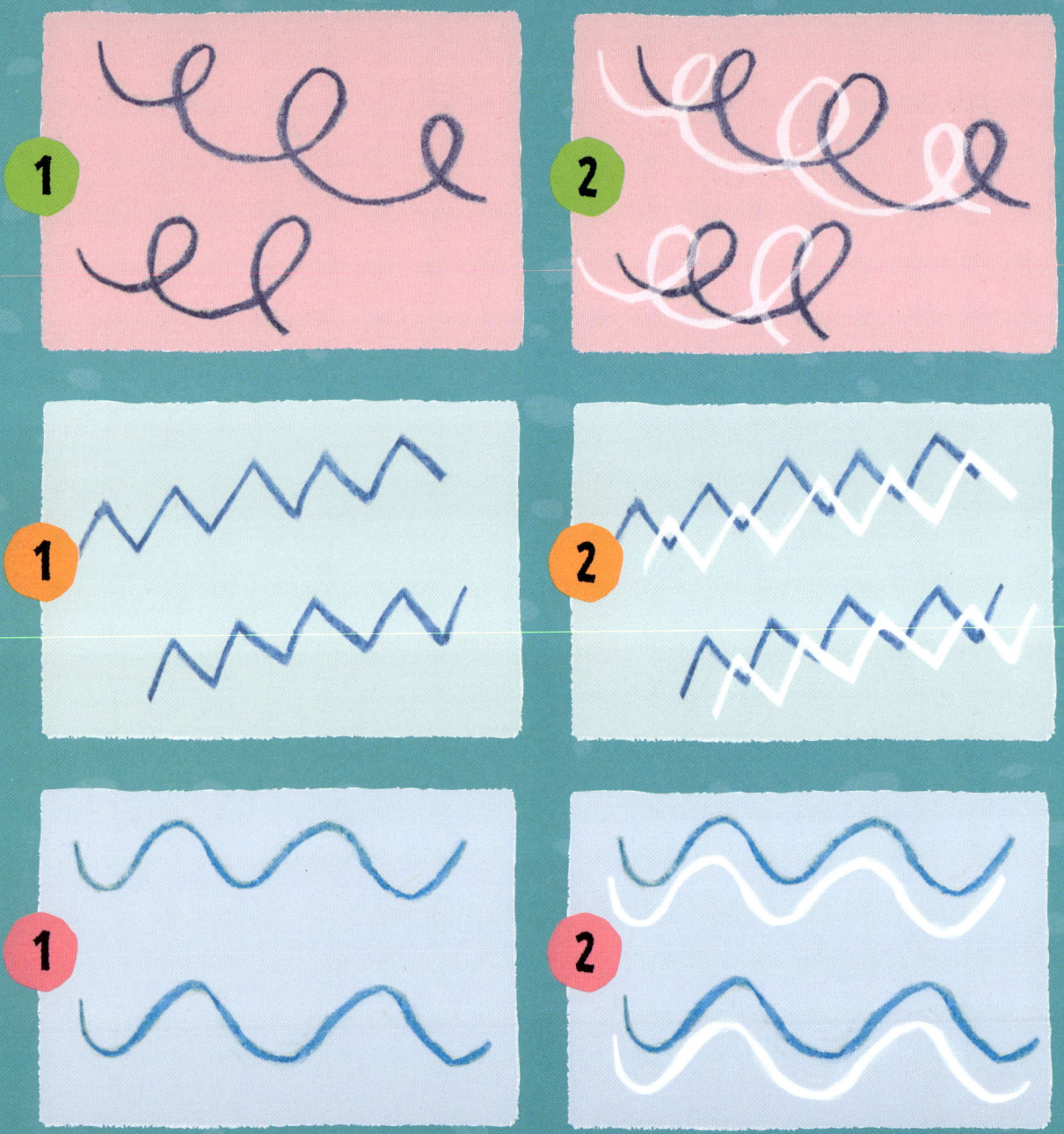

Help these skaters to make cool trails and patterns on the ice!

Snowy Day

Draw your toboggan and a simple figure outline. Fill it in and add a hat and a flying scarf for movement.

Use the blunt end of the crayon to make snowballs. Shade them in evenly or with circular scribbles.

Exquisite Eggs

Try out different striped and dotted patterns to decorate the eggs. Why not add a a cute chick that's just popped out of one?

Draw some beautiful eggs and fluffy chicks for mother hen!

Pumpkin Parade!

Draw banana-shaped lines inside your pumpkin outline. Shade in the orange area lightly, so the mouth and eyes really stand out!

Can you come up with more ideas for spooky faces?

Hooray for Halloween! Add more jack-o'-lantern faces to the parade.

Spooky Party

Woooo! Use the side of the crayon to fill in your ghost. Now, do you want it to be happy—or SCARY? Use really sharp crayons for clear faces!

Party time! Add more fancy-dress spooks dancing to the music.

Munching Monsters

Twist the crayon end inside black circles to make eyes (as many as you like!). Draw in the bodies with faces on top. Use short strokes to draw fur.

Add more hungry monsters to munch on all the party food!

On the Beach

Build up your sandcastle with blocks of yellow and orange, using crayons side-on. Pick out the details carefully with the pointy tips.

For decoration, make simple shell shapes in spirals and fans.

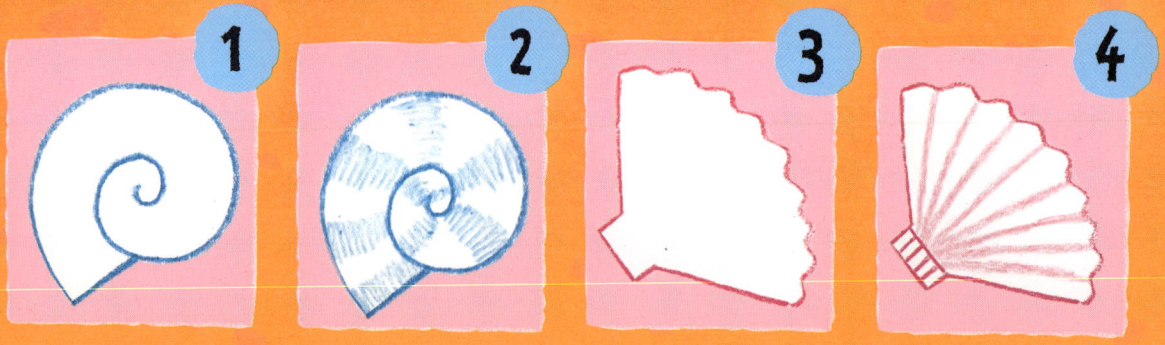

Can you build the biggest sandcastle on the beach? Add seashells and flags too!

Super Surfboards

It's summer! Fill in the surfboard shapes with bright stripes and patterns. Stipple contrasting dots over a plain background.

Let's go surfing! But first make sure everyone has a brightly decorated surfboard.

Panda Pals

Draw a bean-shaped outline. Fill in with white and add a fringe of neck fur using black up-and-down strokes. Extra-short, light strokes give a furry effect.

Add a friend or two for these shy pandas. Give them all some tasty leaves to munch too!

Tiny Tiger

Draw the stripes in strong black before adding orange fur. Finish the fur with short strokes of a darker crayon. Add claws and whiskers in black.

Add a furry tiger cub, bounding through the jungle.

Use shading to make some jungle butterflies!

Happy Hippos

Lay your hippo outline over a textured surface and rub the crayon over it. Add splashes and dots of mud in brown or orange.

What's this? A hippo under the water! Press a little harder to make its shadow.

This glorious mud bath needs some hippos to make a splash. Add them now!

Roarsome Lions!

Draw the lion's outline in orange and fill it in with yellow.
Its mane is just a scribble of spirals!

Who is making all that noise?
It's a "roarsome" lion—draw one in here!

ROOAAARRR!

Zooming Zebras

Fill in the outline in white and overlay details in black. Use the edge of the flat crayon end for fine stripes. Try different leg positions as in Steps 2 and 3.

Let's race! Add more zebras to gallop to the finishing line.

Hanging Around!

Mix a little brown with orange, then add firm, dark strokes at the end for one very hairy orangutan!

Look up there! Add another hairy orangutan, swinging though the branches.

Spot the Cheetah!

Spin a black crayon point on a bright yellow body for the cheetah's spots. Use green and yellow crayons together at an angle to show windswept grass under her feet!

Whoooosh! Add more super-fast, super-spotty cheetahs.

Fluffy Bunnies!

Give your bunny a pattern and an eye patch. Fluff up his fur with dark lines over light brown. Remember his ears are pink inside!

Draw a triangle with the sharp tip of an orange crayon. Fill it in and add details.

It's feeding time. Add more fluffy bunnies—
you'd better add more carrots too!

Crazy Cats

Draw blue outlines and try out some brilliant effects. Stipple dots with the crayon tip, overlay pink on pink or yellow, and scribble bright yellow and green together.

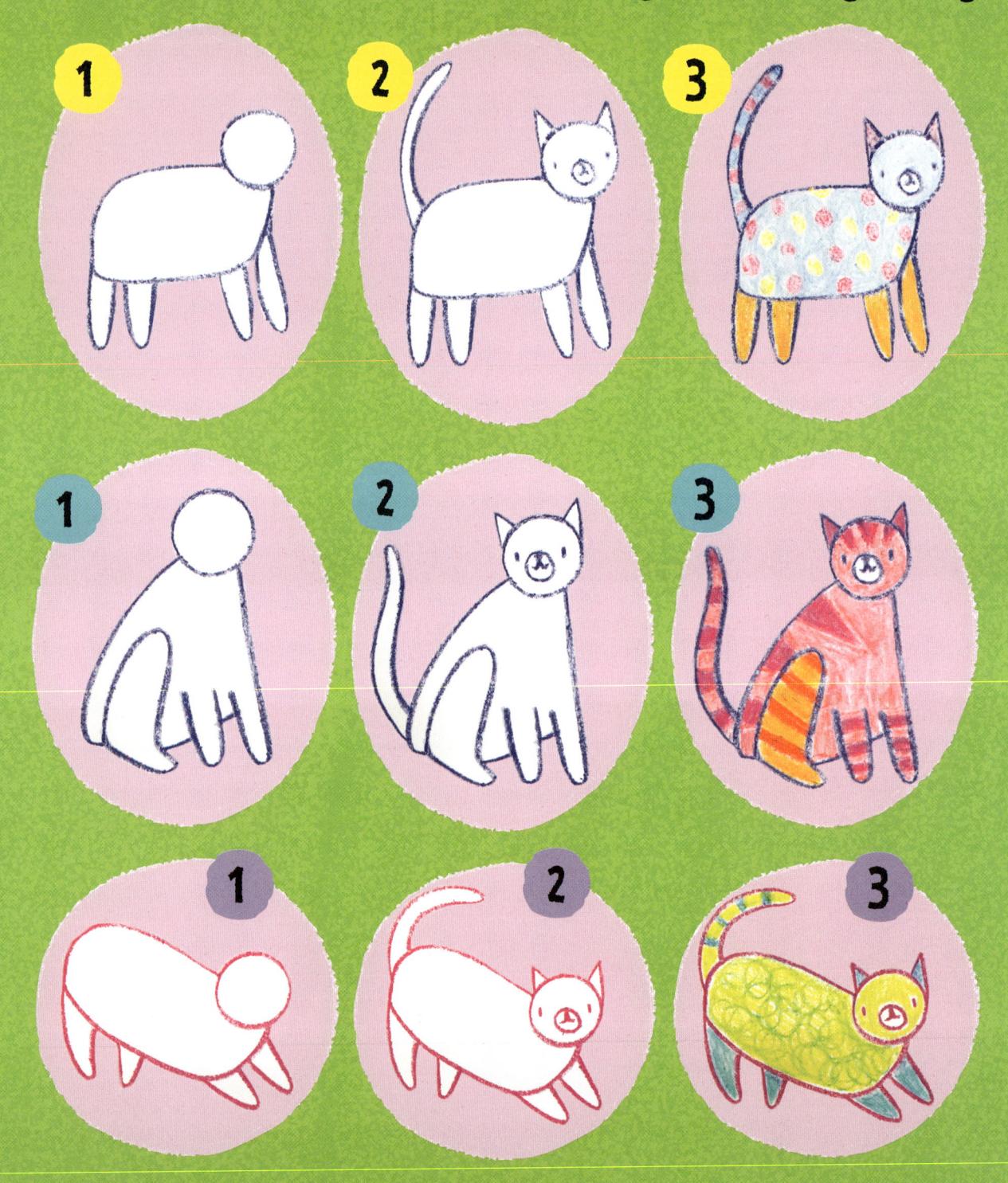

Draw some purr-fectly crazy cats, all different shades and patterns.

Dashing Doggies!

These posh dogs are proud of their fancy knitwear. Fill in the background of each outfit lightly, and overlay with darker stripes, stars, and repeat patterns.

1
2
3
4
5
6

Brrr! It's cold out today. All the doggies are going to need warm coats!

45

Hungry Hamsters

Fill in the outline and add circular scribbles for fluffy fur. Hamsters are busy little things, so add lots of whooshy movement lines!

46

Hamsters are SO cute! Add more furry friends to play with here.

Sleepy Sheep!

Draw a cloud shape. Lay it over a texture, and rub it very gently with a black crayon. Add scribbles on top. Draw more sheep jumping, too!

1
2
3
4
5
6

48

The easy way to get to sleep is by counting lovely lambs! 1,2,3... zzzz.

Ready, Steady, Go!

Make three zooming race cars from different shapes. Add slanted scribble wheels and a driver. Finish with motion lines and they're off!

Add some speedy race cars to the track. Which car will win the race?

High-Flying Helicopter

Use the crayon side-on to show the whirling helicopter blades all in a blur. Add an oval for the body and fill it in. Don't forget the pilot!

1
2
3
4
5

52

Add a hovering helicopter in the sky.

Mighty Trucks

Put two simple blocks together and you have a truck. Fill it in, leaving a square window and a circle to show what's inside. Add wheels, a driver, and lights!

Add some big trucks with brightly painted sides.
What are they carrying?

Construction Site

Fill in the dump truck with a side-on yellow crayon. Add darker lines for the ridged side. Rub the earth mover over a bumpy metal surface. Make the wheels and track with the round end of a black crayon and finish them off with short strokes.

Add some tough vehicles to get the job done on the construction site. Get to work now!

Monster Trucks

Merge a layer of yellow, orange, and red. Cover with a thick layer of black. Use a sharp pencil to scrape off two flame shapes. Add wheels and you're ready to go!

1.
2.
3.
4.
5.

Add more monster trucks with cool paint jobs!

Night Drivers

Use varying pressure to fill in the car shape. Use the flat end of a black crayon for the wheels and add a yellow triangle for the lights.

It's time to go home. Fill the highway with cars—make sure they have their headlights switched on.

All Aboard!

Draw two long parallel lines for a track, then fit short parallel lines in between them. Draw the green train, and add scribble wheels. Make its steam by twirling a crayon end.

1

2

3

4

Choo! Choo! Add a train and more track and climb aboard!

To the Rescue!

An "L"-shape on its side makes a neat fire truck. Add details in black, and a flashing light. Don't forget dashes to show that it is shining. This is an emergency!

Quick, help to rescue this silly cat. Draw in a fire truck—make sure it's got a long ladder!

MEOW!

Tractor Trails

Fill in the cab shape with a texture rubbing, using the crayon side-on. The field is another texture rubbing in orange with double crayon lines added.

Help the farmer in the field.
Add a tractor and make some tracks!

Up and Away!

Use the tip of the crayon to make fine lines for the balloon patterns.
Fill in the spaces loosely in any combination you like.

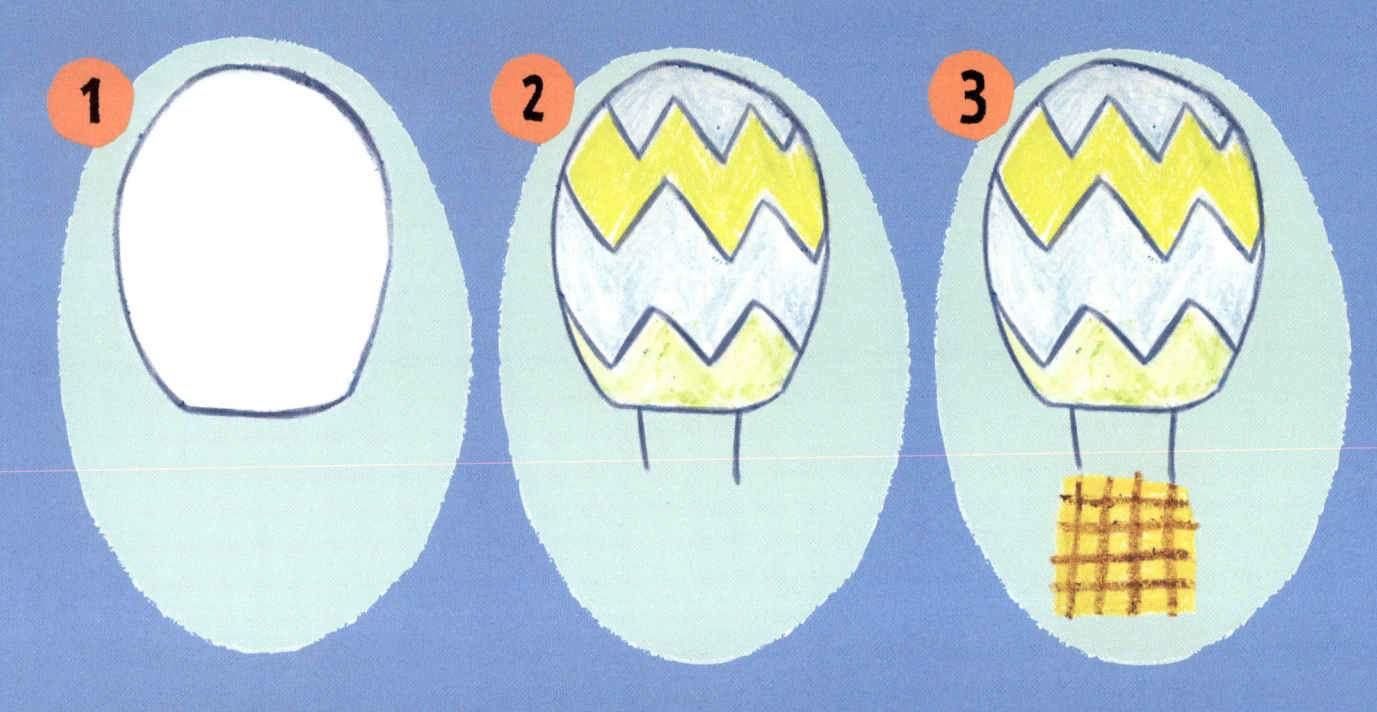

1 2 3

Criss-cross a block of yellow with brown or orange lines for the basket.

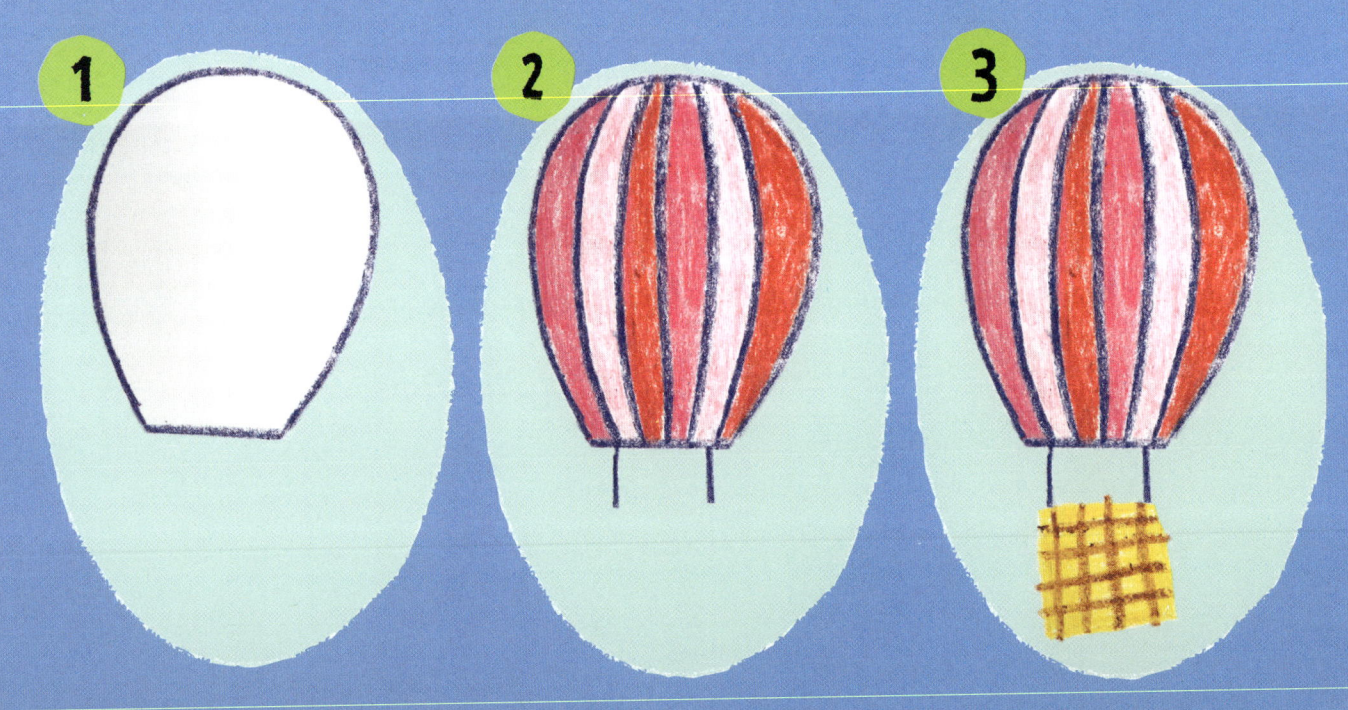

1 2 3

68

Fill the skies with amazing balloons.
Give them stripes or bright patterns.

Air Show!

Add wings and small triangles to a larger triangle. Shade them in lightly and add details in red, and then a blue cockpit. Don't forget double lines for jet trails!

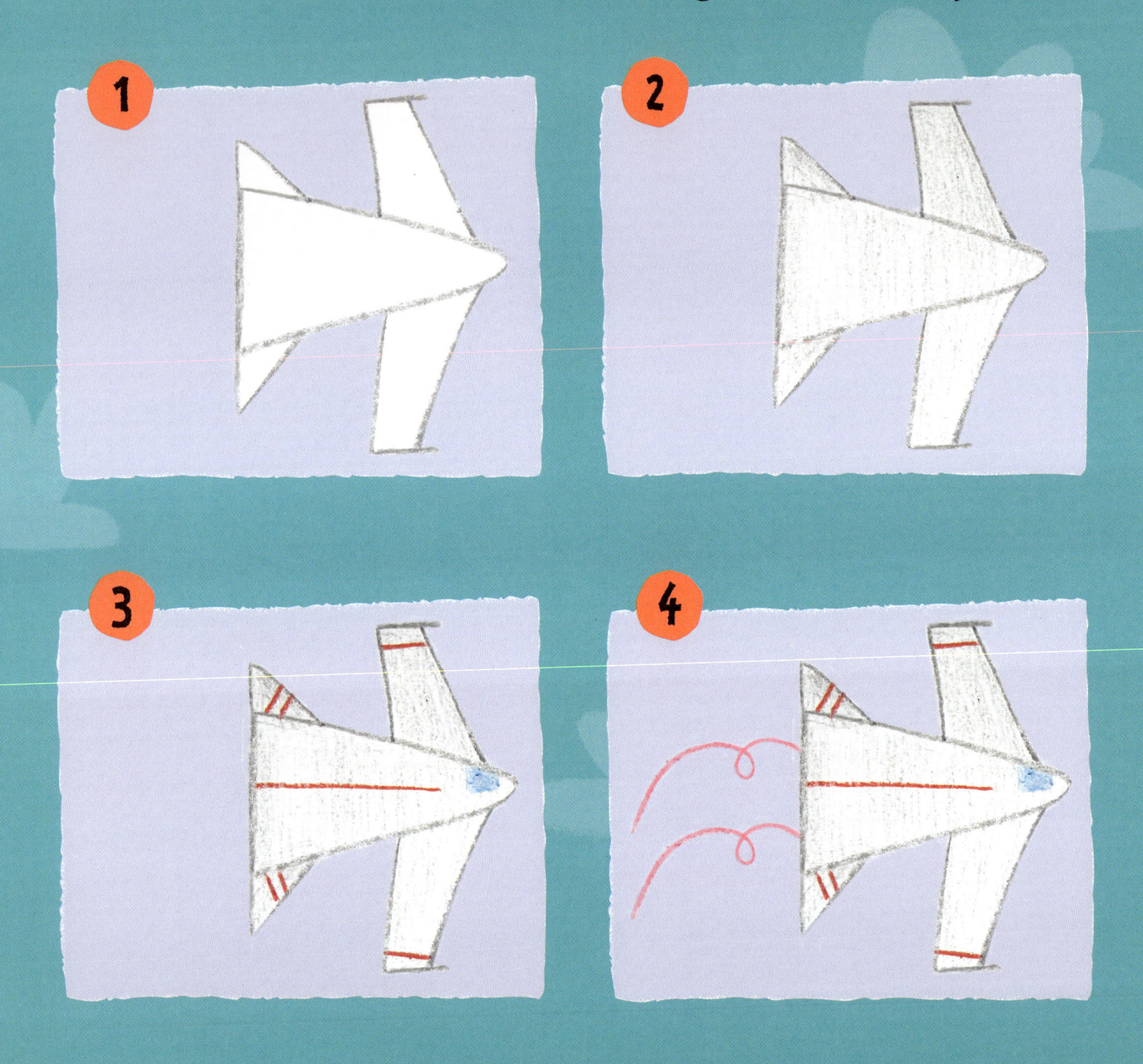

Zoom! Zoom! Add another shiny jet plane to the air show display!

Super Space Rocket

Shade the rocket in blue with details in black. The happy astronaut is waiting for blast-off. Mix red, orange, and yellow for the flames—and she's away!

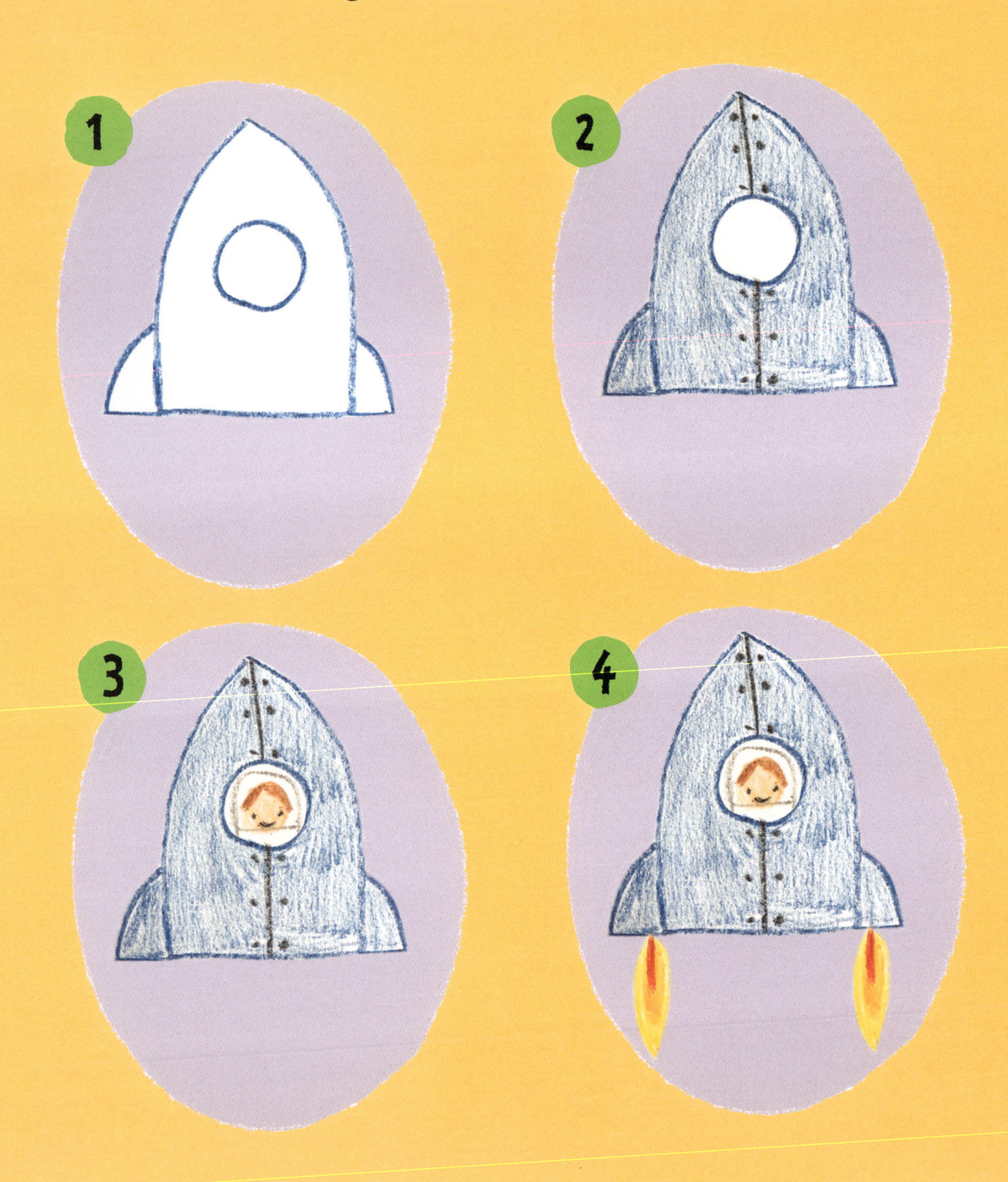

Get ready for blast off! Add a rocket ready to leave this planet.

Penguin Parade

Fill in the top of the penguin carefully in black, leaving two little dots for eyes. Add a yellow beak and feet. She's waving a flag!

1
2
3
4
5

Now draw her baby—he's much lighter, with a different face and black feet.

1
2
3

Add more penguins to the parade.
Give some of them flags to wave about!

Splashing About!

Make a wavy sea by rubbing the page over a texture like bark. Add darker ripples with paired crayons. Fill in the whale in a dark blue, and add its waterspout last.

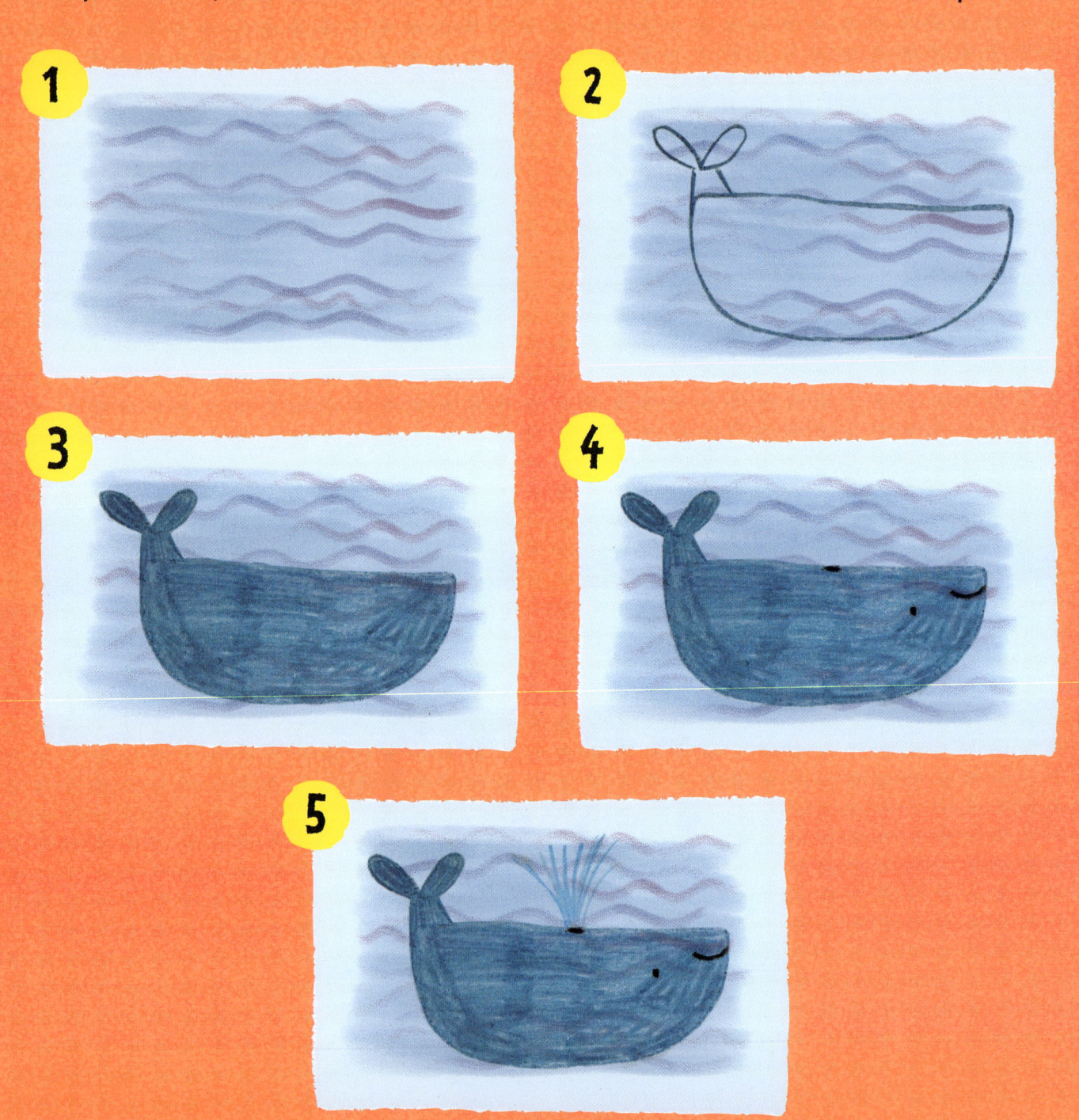

Whales love playing with water. Add more whales splashing about, having fun at sea.

Friends Forever!

Sea otters are a bit spoon-shaped! Fill in with brown leaving an oval for his tummy. Add details in black, and two-tone ripples. He's having a lovely time floating about!

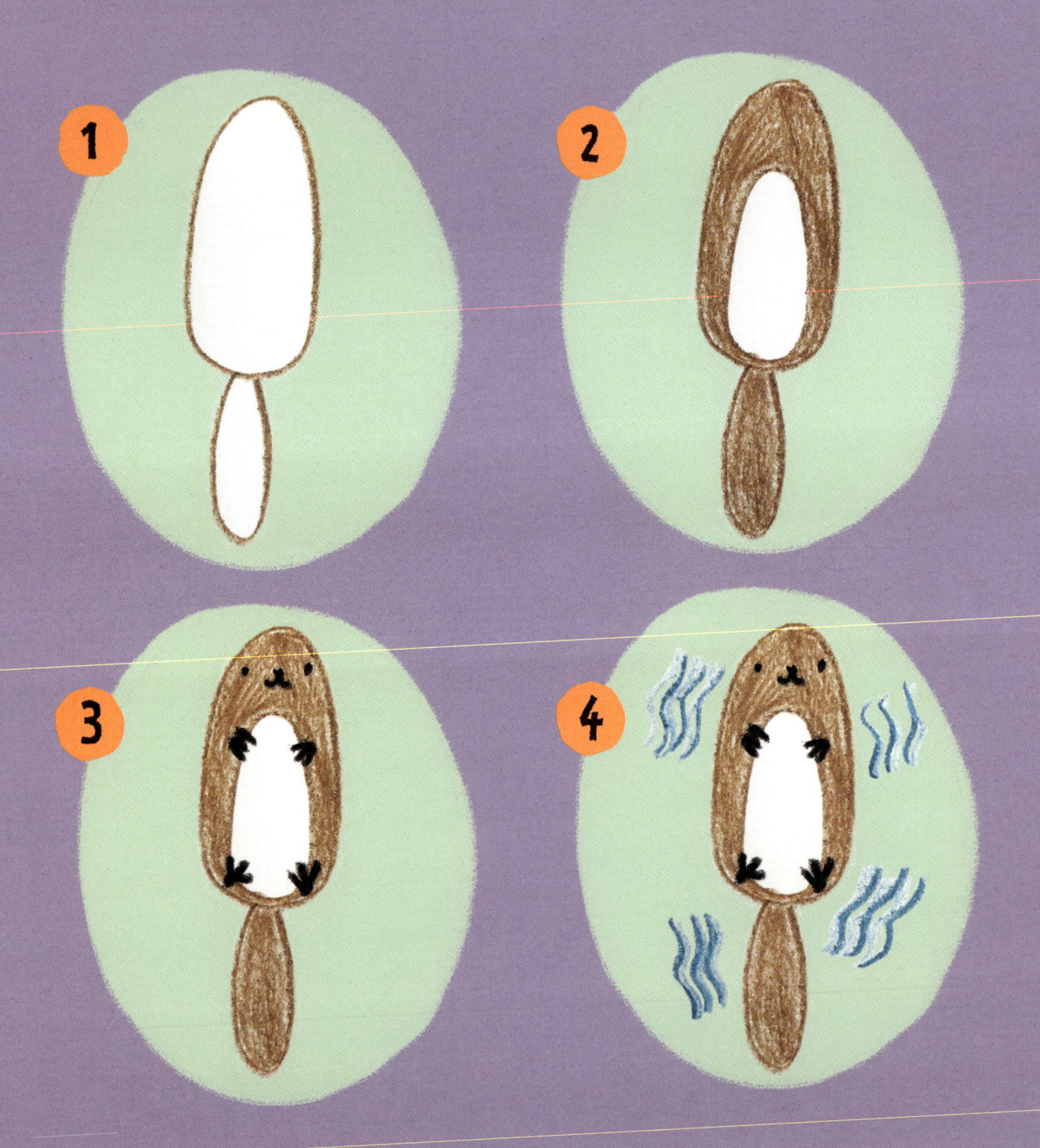

1

2

3

4

Add more friendly sea otters. Otters hold hands when they sleep, so they don't drift away from each other!

Super Swimmers!

Begin with a semi-circle, add the turtle's swimming body, then have fun decorating its shell. Use stipple dots, criss-cross lines, and red triangles over yellow.

1
2
3
4

Add more tiny turtles with fantastic shells to this swim trip.

Beach Games!

Build up from an oval and add claws and eye stalks. Fill in with red and orange, then add pupils and a smile with the point of a black crayon—and he's ready to play!

1

2

3

4

5

This little crab wants to play beach volleyball.
Add some friends for him to play with!

Undersea Explorers!

Etch out some super sea life! Overlay a light layer with a darker one, and use a safe, pointed tool to draw some friendly ocean creatures.

Add incredible sea creatures to spot through the porthole of the submarine.

Fantastic Fish!

Tropical fish have brilliant patterns! Copy how they look by twisting a crayon point over shading, adding dots and stripes, and drawing looped lines to look like scales.

Add more amazing fish to the coral reef.
Make them bright to match their surroundings!

Dolphin Race

Draw a dolphin or two with different expressions in black. Vary the crayons you choose, too. Don't forget the ripples as they leap out of the water!

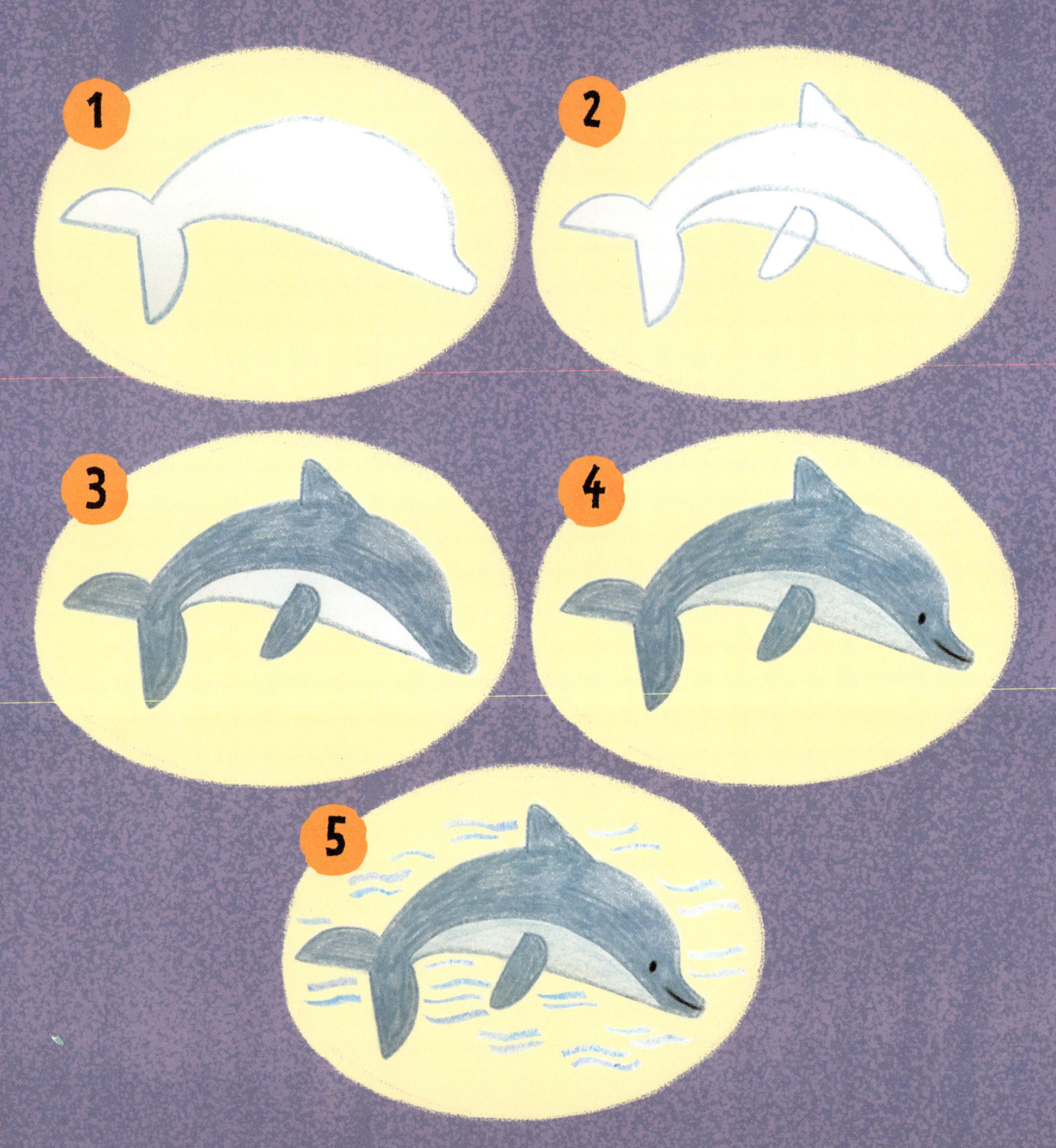

1
2
3
4
5

Add more speedy dolphins, leaping and racing to the finish line.

Speeding Along!

Draw a simple boat shape and add your own figures. Pick out the waves in darker lines and don't forget the spray from the speeding skier!

How can you ski without snow?
It's easy with a speedboat and some water skis!

Deep Sea Disco

One circle and eight tentacles make an octopus! Get them in a disco mood with bright pink and lime green. Add strong dots for their suckers.

1.
2.
3.
4.

Add more octopuses with amazing dance moves to this deep-sea dance floor.

Sail into the Sunset

Add a bright blue sail and pink flag to a simple boat shape. Then draw others and decorate them differently to make a whole flotilla of pretty boats.

Rub blue and pink crayons over a textured surface for the sunset sky.

Add more sailing boats to this scene. Give them bright sails and fluttering flags. Show a lovely sunset, too!

Special Delivery!

It's Christmas Eve—time to deliver some presents. All you need to do is draw Santa and his sack of toys!